TRANSMIT
TRUE AND BRIGHTLY

POETRY OF
NANCY SUMMERS

By Nancy Summers

Edited by John-Brian Paprock

TRANSMIT TRUE AND BRIGHTLY: POETRY OF NANCY SUMMERS

By Nancy Summers

Edited by John-Brian Paprock

Design and photography by John-Brian Paprock

Some photographs are from family collection

Copyright 2018: John-Brian Paprock

Published by Holy Transfiguration Publications

P. O. Box 22352, Minneapolis, Minnesota 55422

ISBN 978-0-578-20697-4

To stand in crystal solitude

And send a golden ray

Rainbow riding.

Glancing, gliding

Out into the day

To transmit true and brightly

All light that shows

That you are there.

Miriam (Nancy Summers)
Journal 1980

Transmit True and Brightly

Contents

Transmit True and Brightly

Summers Daughter

"We are all going home" written in a journal of Nancy Summers, dated March 1980.

Born on the summer solstice in 1940 in Oak Park, Illinois, Nancy Jean Summers grew up in the middle class of middle America, truly Summers daughter. She had several legal surname changes over the years by marriage: Paprock, Roderick, Koehl. Her most precious name change was not legal but from adult baptism: Miriam.

By the time Nancy graduated Oak Park High School in 1958, she had a few poems published. Nancy loved the theater arts and was very involved in high school drama productions. Even so, she was primarily a musician. Her talent as a cellist gained her a scholarship to the prestigious Chautauqua Institution. Nancy could play a variety of instruments, enjoyed them all, but she loved her vocal instrument. She could sing in all the languages of classic opera. In the late 1960s, she sang with Bill Russo's opera in Chicago. One of my fondest memories from my childhood is her singing, playing

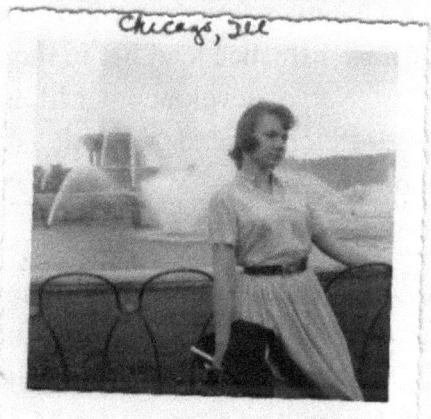

Overlooking Des Plaines River

July 1959

Chicago, Ill

guitar and piano.

Nancy's love of the arts eventually led her to the community of Taliesin, where artists, musicians and writers were invited to participate in Frank Lloyd Wright's holistic and innovative architectural school in Spring Green, Wisconsin.

Young Nancy had the opportunity to head to Taliesin West in Arizona with Frank Lloyd Wright's Russian wife. Even though Nancy's formal relationship with Taliesin was short, it had a major impact in her life. She stayed in the West, going to the coast of California. Nancy always maintained a deep spiritual connection with the ideals of Taliesin.

Drawn to the mysteries of the universe and of human relations, Nancy (and a few of her closest friends, Linda and Ardis) began exploring paths where spiritual development and artistic expression converged. Among her explorations included the writings of George Gurdjieff, Carl Jung, Dion Fortune, among others. At the end of the 1950s, Nancy participated in a few sessions hosted by a gentleman she affectionately called "Mr. Gilroy." Such respect she had for him that she never referred by any other name. Through this man's influence (and her own insatiable curiosity), she eventually studied western esoteric, mystical and occult, systems. She developed skills in astrology, palmistry and other divinatory arts. But Mr. Gilroy's greatest influence lead her to the Russian Orthodox Church. This is where Nancy developed her lifelong love of the Orthodox Church and a lifelong friendship with a devout Christian mystic, Maryangela Toombs, who was active in the American Mission of the Russian Orthodox Church.

Among the artists, musicians and poets she encountered then, she met several friends and lovers, including one that could have been her husband. Later in her life, she loved to tell the stories of her amorous and spiritual adventures as a young woman.

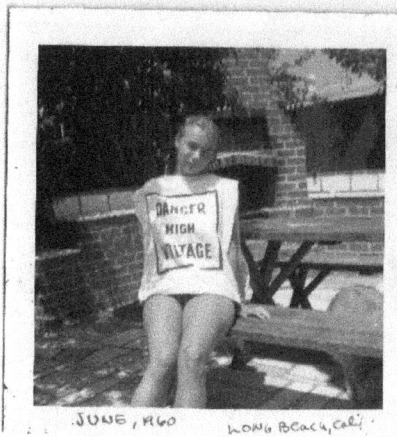

JUNE, 1960   LONG BEACH, Cal.

At one the parties the Taliesin folk would attend in Southern California, she met an art student – Kenneth Paprock – and fell in love. By July 26, 1960, she was married in Tlaquiltenango Morales, south of Mexico City in Mexico. The young couple would return to Mexico City the following year, where I was born.

Two more children (Dara and Matthew) were born in Southern California before Nancy and Kenneth were able to move back to the Land of Lincoln where she was born. In Chicago, the stormy marriage to Kenneth eventually succumbed to the winds of change. They were divorced in 1968.

Richard Roderick, Nancy's second husband, was supposed to be her soul mate. He accepted Nancy with her three children and took them from near poverty in Chicago to a large house in River Forest. Nancy and Richard were in 1968. In 1969, at the Apollo 11 splash down, she gave birth to her fourth child (August). Nancy wanted her new life to be spiritually protected and preserved – and so, she and her River Forest family were baptized in the Orthodox Christian Church that same year.

Her soul mate union seemed like everything Nancy wanted, but it was disrupted by the lifestyle changes of the late 1960s. Trust became an elusive commodity in their relationship. Nancy's mother agreed to take the children in her home in Nevada while she and Richard tried to work things out. Instead, she arrived in Nevada devastated by a broken relationship and very pregnant. She gave birth at the end of 1971. Her fifth child, Benjamin, died in December, never leaving the hospital.

The depth of her grief was so deep, so hard for anyone to fully understand, including herself. She began a period of heavy drinking. There is no poetry from the end of 1970 until 1973 – from Chicago, Illinois to Henderson, Nevada to Berkeley, California and, finally, to Madison, Wisconsin.

Although Nancy travelled, Madison was the home she had been looking for. By the mid-1970s, she was treated for her alcoholism and married the love of her life, William (Bill) Koehl. Roots were laid down at a house at the end of Harley Drive on the southwest edge of Madison, a house with a large garden and fruit trees. Bill made sure that she was nurtured by love as he made sure the garden was tended. Accordingly, he made sure that her music was alive. For many years, Nancy had been without her favorite instruments. So, Bill bought her a cello and a piano for their home and, for the years that followed, music never left.

In the 1980s, Nancy was diagnosed with breast cancer. In a few years, she battled that disease to a remission. In her 40s, she completed her own college degree in nutritional science at the University of Wisconsin. Nancy held a professional position as a clinical nutritionist at Mendota Mental Health Institute for years.

The 1980s also brought Nancy's close high school friends (Ardis and Linda) to join her in building a church community in Madison, the Holy Transfiguration Orthodox Mission. Nancy played the organ for the small Sunday liturgy and sang joyfully the Orthodox hymns. Her devotion was deep and sometimes profound. Even so, her husband claimed he was an atheist for many of the years of the Mission. Bill supported her anyway and Nancy's faith sustained them both. When Bill started moving toward the end of his own life, he converted and was baptized in a private ceremony. Bill passed way in 1988 from an enlarged heart.

By 1991, regular Orthodox Christian services for Holy Transfiguration community that Nancy was devoted were suspended due to lack of active clergy.

Shortly after that, although she did not mention it to anyone at the time, her cancer returned. She began drinking and smoking. Keeping a brave face, Nancy was able to reach sobriety again and joined another Orthodox Christian community in the Madison area.

Despite the pain of bone lesions and an occasional morphine fog, she took pleasure in giving piano lessons to her grandchildren. Her writing, however, became sparse. During her last years, there was no written poetry, but she made cassette tapes for her children, with poetry and music.

Nancy died July 15, 2000. The legacy of her words continues.

Notes about this collection

There has been a deliberate attempt to preserve the poetry of Nancy Summers in the manner and form of the writing as she left it.

This is not the first time for an attempt to collect her writings. Nancy wanted to have her poems typed and gathered from the scraps of paper and journals she kept, but always seemed to leave them in a box. She would just throw hand-written scraps of poetry on top. In 1974, I gathered her writings and, in secret, spent months learning to type. Then, using a neighbor's typewriter and kitchen, I typed her poems into a two and a half volume collection of her poetry. I even drew some illustrations and covers for them. The poems were divided by year and decade: into I. for the 1950s and II. for the 1960s; with a third volume started for the 1970s. Nancy added a few type-written poems to the last volume, but it is unclear why she did not maintain that. She started a journal for the 1980s but did not maintain it either.

For Christmas in 1974, Nancy was surprised with the gift of her poetry. Typing in secret had a drawback, she was unable to edit. After Nancy passed away, I inherited her poetry and found she made edits and changes to a few of the poems that I typed so many years before. The volumes were never reproduced.

The current collection, intending to be as comprehensive as possible, utilizes scans of some of those 1974 typed pages as well as scans a few hand-written poems. In addition, included are scans of a few of the newer poems Nancy added to the third volume. The rest of her writings were hand-written. These were typed (or re-typed) and also included in this collection.

The basic presentation of this collection is divided into important locations of Nancy's life for periods of time that are not easily divided into years and decades. I hope this allows her poetry to better speak for her. The chapter divisions also help in managing the quantity of poems included in this book. An index of poem titles or first lines (for untitled poems) has been added as well.

Chapter 1. Land of Lincoln: This chapter begins with a poem Nancy wrote when she was 13 years old. The chapter is named for Nancy's childhood home in Illinois, born and raised in Oak Park. This is the beginning of her sojourn through the world with poetry.

Chapter 2. Taliesin: This chapter includes poetry from the time after graduating Oak Park High School. Nancy took a few years to find her direction.

Chapter 3. Southern California: This chapter includes poetry from her young adult hood when she engaged the world through marriage with the birth of three children. Nancy was part of the arts community in Southern California, while her husband was a graduate student at UCLA.

Chapter 4. Chicagoland: This chapter includes poetry after her return to the Midwest. This was a turbulent time when she married her second husband. The Chicagoland chapter concludes at the beginning of a period of great turmoil in her life.

Chapter 5. Mad-City: This chapter includes poetry from the end of Nancy's alcoholic haze in Madison, Wisconsin.

Chapter 6. Edge of Fitchburg: This chapter includes poetry from Nancy's final home, a place she found with her soul mate, her third husband. It also includes poetry of her religious and spiritual devotion.

Chapter 7. Places of Light: This chapter includes the few poems and prose Nancy wrote as the end of her life neared. In these, the depth of her spiritual connection can be felt.

By the way, it is clear to me that this is not a complete collection. My mother was known to give away her hand-written poetry when moved by a connection or an encounter. There is a story that my mother, Nancy, would tell of sharing her poetry at parties in Southern California, an intersection of the arts community and the folk music scene in the mid-1960s. She met several important singers, including Joni Mitchell. Nancy wrote the words, reportedly, that are sung in Joni's iconic song "Clouds (Both Sides Now)." She reflected on the gift she gave Joni, but never in anger. She was not disheartened that she was not given credit, saying, "I gave her the poem." Her gifts of poetry are considered precious treasures to friends and lovers and family. I made no attempt to gather these gifts for this collection.

In addition to her original hand-written poems and the edited and typed versions, there are some poems that seemed to be written more than once, but with some changes. Because Nancy kept both editions, some of these are also included.

As I put this together, I daydreamed about scholars and historians finding in these pages, in these poems, insight from a truly American life and placing her writing in its rightful place in American literature.

It is my hope this collection will be treasured by those who knew her, loved her, experienced her – as a gift from Nancy herself.

For everyone else, it is my hope that her words will inspire and tickle you; reach your heart and your soul and help you soar above; that you will get to know an amazing, intelligent, witty, deeply spiritual human being and child of God.

Compare these editions:

26 May 1961

Alpha

Through a scarlet screaming night
Gemini shone silent
In the first hours of the sign.
Mercury soared to tell the sky
Of life so early torn from dark
Deep in the womb
And then a breath – a softened cry
A man-child met the dawn.

26 May 1961

22 May 1991

Beneath the wings of Quetzlcoatl
In the mountain city of Tenochtitlan
Mercury rose before the Light
To tell the sky of Life
So early torn from Dark
Deep in the womb.
Red Rivers ran before my eyes
A heavenly decision made
To stay on earth this time –
And then first breath
Soft Ancient Cry
Sun-Child met the dawn.

5/22/61

Mexico City, D.F.

(sent in birthday card 5/22/91)

Cover art from the 1974 collection of Nancy Summers poetry

Land of Lincoln

Transmit True and Brightly

Transmit True and Brightly

I Remember

I

I remember a springtime

A May as rich and rare

When every bird was singing

Every blossom full and fair

I remember music

Too sweet for mortal ear

And I remember breezes whispering

That told me heaven was near

I remember a concert

When I first met him (may 2)

I'd rather not say his name

So let's call him Jim

I remember a feeling

Which I'd never had before

The feeling I had for Jimmy

That drilled right to the core

II

I remember Jim

He was a sailor and

I remember too, a wedding,

But just make believe I'm glad

III

I remember singing

The songs that angels sing

In a chorus filled with wonder

Such as only Jim could bring

IV

I remember a track meet

That was held inside

Jim didn't win first place

But better still he tried

I remember after that track meet

When my heart felt as light as foam

And Jeannie told him something
And Jimmy rode me home!

I remember mother
Who helped me find my way
And I remember hopping with him
On that beautiful spring day

V

I remember the second day
Of that great track meet
And he only came in third because
He didn't try to cheat

I remember Jeannie
Giving Jim her ring
And he asked for my ring too
For the luck that it would bring

I remember kissing it
To give him a surprise
And when Nancy told him there was more

I read questions in Jim's eyes

I remember my heart leaping
Much higher than I reckoned!
I prayed and kept my fingers crossed
And this time, Jim came in second!

I remember walking home
With Jim and Nancy
It wasn't very far

I remember a tingle
When he put his hand on mine
I remember when he pressed it hard
Those shivers up my spine

I remember Nancy taking the bike
'Cause Jim forgot his shoes
He wanted me to go with him
I had not a thing to love

I remember saying
"Don't look at me that way!"
And I remember him saying

"It's a much different way today'

I remember after
He had changed the tire
I remember the way he watched me
Made my breath turn to fire.

I remember telling myself
That this just couldn't be
Everyone knew he loved Johnnie
Was he just fooling me?

I remember behind the church
Looking into eyes of blue
I told him all my troubles
It was like a dream come true.

May 12, 1954

To Us

Say au revoir but not good-bye
Though May is past, love will not die
The past is gone,

But memory gives

One clinging thought,

"The future lives!"

Our duty first love must not lead

What might have been

Had fate decreed

'twere better for had we not met

I loved you then I love you yet

The fairest May is living still –

A rippling laugh, a word at will

So let's forget what others say

My love is stronger than it was in May.

To the Boy Scouts,

Two little Girl Scouts, sisters were they

Selling Girl Scout cookies on a gray March day

Their feet were all swollen and black and blue

And if you had to sell cookies yours would be too!

They trampled up and down the street with a sigh

Trying to find people to buy cookies. And why?

Because they were true Girl Scouts,

A spirit I had then

That no one else had on that cold March day.

By Nancy Summers,
A tired girl scout

Eyes

There are eyes of blue like an autumn sky

There are eyes of brown like a fawn so shy

There are eyes as black as a raven's nest;

There are eyes of grey like the silvery rain,

There are hazel eyes like a wooded lane,

But those soft green eyes, I love the best.

Why is it that little trees huddle together?

They all look alike and they huddle together, together

A lone little tree could be just as a feather

In wind and high weather, high weather, high weather

Lest the tap root be deep where it fastens the feather,

Fastens the feather, the feather, the feather

There is sunlight to grow in along the heather

There's time to rejoice when you've conquered the heather, the heather, the heather

Why is it that little trees live all together?

Their branches entangle and die close together, together,

They lean different ways, but the roots are together,

They all look alike and they die on the heather,

And they die close together, together, together,

Together.

QUERY

O God of reason tell me
How one poor heart will know
It's mate; the while be searching for
A diamond in the snow.

O God of Mercy answer
Through youth's bright melody
O where is there a partner for
A heart born to be free?

O God of God eternal
Before time Thou hast known
That some hearts find their places and
Some brave Life's storm alone.

29 January 1957

MAY

If by some chance I had the pow'rs
To make one dream come true
I'd wish for May's bright happy hours
To last the whole year through.

For May is love that soars and sings
And Maytime blooms with youth
An echo of her music rings
With innocence and truth.

I would that May were all year long
That I might ever hear
Her cheerful note her laughing song
And keep my heaven near

5 March 1957

A HEART THAT'S FREE

A gypsy's life is the life for me
A foot that's loose and a heart that's free
A blue sky above and bright sunshine
A warm west wind and the world is mine.

I'll whistle a tune and then I'll hum
And people I pass will think I'm "dumb"
But I don't care 'cause I'm just me
And have no cares for my heart is free.

So as soon as spring bursts into bloom
I'll go my way for it's surely doom
To settle down. Yes I must be
Where my foot is loose and my heart is free.

12 March 1957

MATURITY

How sad when I passed girlhood by
Leaving it far behind
The careless joys of childhood play
Never again to find.

Heavy the heart of maiden kind
Finding life   not so fair
                 when knowing less
Had never a doubt or care.

Sorry the soul when May is gone
Followed by stately June
Not so sad that spring has fled
But summer's come so soon.

Peace is the song that Summer sings
Whispering low to each
Though blossoms fade and gently fall
There hangs the ripening peach.

17 April 1957

REMERCIE

You mean the world to me,
Yet I would not die without you;
For through your strength of soul
I gain that inward light
That wins my battles.

You are the world to me,
Yet should you leave
I would not shed a tear;
For you have taught well the lesson
Of living with a burden
Without the sense of martyrdom
And self-pity,
Of being only glad for everlasting youth--
One cherished memory!

20 June 1957

ANTICIPATION

It's the fall of the year
And out on the pier
A brisk breeze is blowing the sun=gilded leaves
Over the lake.

His hand touches mine
And as fingers entwine
A glimpse of the beauty we've yet to enjoy
Reaches my heart . . . . . .

And I pray.

10 October 1957

MIRAGE

I gaze out the window
And watch the whirling snowflakes
Dash across the frosty pane.

The wind speaks to my eager heart
And a clutching fear strikes me--
"EEK! This is Arizona!"

21 October 1957

TWO THINGS

Of all the treasures that earth holds in store
Two things are most precious to me--
A boy with a yearning to sail 'round the world
And a man navigating Life's sea.

With feverish youth running swift in his veins
A boy ran away with my heart;
But a man smiling wisely through all my mistakes
Had captured my love from the start.

There's only one thing in this world that compares
With a boy--only one thing that can--
'Tis his time-mellowed image that finally comes
When a boy grows into a man.

November 1957

Consciousness

Who can foretell the destiny of man?

The knowledge lies within us,

Locked against our sleeping selves,

Buried alive!

The key is hidden in the clutter of daily life

And if found may be thrown aside

For lack of that certain door

Rotting with age.

We are rushing toward self-destruction.

Act!

But act with wisdom.

Find that shining key to knowledge

And live accordingly –

Aware.

2 December 1957

EN ROUTE

Black trees against a cloudy sky
And only mist between us--
Like wind across the field we fly
And not a soul has seen us.

We won't be stopped by worldly things;
Our mission is much greater.
(A sadder song the sparrow sings
And spring will come much later.)

We steal away in foggy dawn,
And in the town behind us
They find that two they loved are gone
And no one dares come find us.

The riddle last had been unwound,
The doors had opened wide--
We dropped our crosses to the ground
And hand in hand we died.

20 December 1957

CLIMAX

It's an adventure
From the bottom--
A hill so very high
That speaking to the sky
Would be simple
At the summit.

It's pure labor
Halfway up the side
My torso wants to drag
And rest on every crag of
Solid flesh
Along the way

Its oblivion
At the top;
But the brilliance of it burns
Until my consciousness returns
To lift my weary thighs to my reward--
Another higher hill. . .
And steeper.

                              25 January 1958

PERPETUUM MOBILE

The vague unrest
That keeps us wand'ring
Calls the traveler
On forever,
Commands the leaders
Of the nations,
Coaxes villians into evil,
Spurs the actor
To his glory.

The far-off voice
That keeps us groping
Tells the artist
All in beauty,
Whispers in the
Ear of madness,
In gentle tones inspires the poet,
And finally leads us
Home to Heaven.

3 February 1958

ODE TO AGONIE IN THE HEDDE

Ah thou heddache! Blasted fiende!
Gette thee gone awaye frome me.
When ofte I have harde taskes to doe,
Thee, thou ratte, arte bye mye syde.

The feaveres, chylles ande sneezelettes,
The broken legges and armpittes
Are naught besyde thye sharpe paine
Thou cruele throbbing monstre plague!

11 March 1958

ONE

I cannot speak of desert skies
I cannot write of warm strong arms
I cannot tell how setting sun and starry nights
Are deep engraved upon my heart.

I cannot whisper of our love. . .
I cannot think of you
In words.

                    28 April 1958

FOLLY

Tall golden stallion
Racing in the wind
Youth fire life
Coursing through your veins
Snorting in defiance
Pawing silver sands
Anxious to be off
Across the timeless hills.

Slender golden stallion
Standing all alone
Shining like a statue
In the morning sun
An unseen crown on that fine head
A kingdom under those black hooves
Yet freedom's call at break of day
Bids you follow fleeting clouds.

1 May 1958

AT TANI DERI

This day started early
With freshness all it's own
Cool damp breeze at morning
Awoke my heart
As I stepped out the door

This day sun is winking
On dewey new-born leaves
Life surrounds my senses
And lilacs bloom

This day I shall try

6 May 1958

AT HILLSIDE

Will you run down the path to meet me
And call my name with joy
When miles have stretched between us
And we've gone separate ways?

Will your arms be happy, warm and strong,
Your eyes still sparkle blue,
When time has laid a cooling hand
On fevered brows of youth?

Will you be glad to walk beside me
When paths converge again--
And learn to sing and laugh once more
Will you love me then?

30 May 1958

WHAT

What can I do for you?
How can I help?
Be your friend
Be your lover
Or what?
I could leave
To start all over
Each of us.
But no--that would be
No answer.
You don't even know
Your name.
That's it--
I can help you find your name.
When you know who you are
Things will be different
Then you'll love me
Or will you hate me?
No, you'll love me
Because you'll wish
I were here.
But I'll be far away
By then.

6 June 1958

Transmit True and Brightly

Taliesin

Transmit True and Brightly

A fine bright day
And green hills
Of black dirt
Left you toward
The day's work
Then the woman
Sick with superiority
And dreams of being God says,
"How's your conscience?"
Suddenly the Sun is Black,
Oh, but you remember
She is sick
She thinks she's God
If I took what she said
As true, I'd become sick
With her
This is so
But how is your conscience man?
How is your conscience boy?
You've your family, friends
And a girl who loves you
And your life hasn't
Even started yet. . .
How is your conscience, Man?

26 July 1958

NEVER OR EVER

Transient. . .
Will we ever come back to today?
I think not.
We either climb or fall.
If we fall
We fall apart
And roll along the valley
On ever diverging paths.
If we climb
We climb the hill together.
The road narrows
Toward the summit
And we must walk single file
One going a step ahead
To help the other
Up!
And reach the top
To find a higher hill to mount
But first go down
To begin the climb once more.
This new hill--
Will we climb again
Or Fall?
Hold tight my hand
We need each other's strength to climb
And we'll climb.

                              3 August 1958

SOMETHING STAYS

To meet and say goodbye--
Yet something stays.
An hour or two
With you,
Perhaps a few days;
It doesn't matter that we met
In a short time
May not even remember
Your face
Or what you said.
Yet something's changed;
Something's been created;
Something stays
Although we never meet
Again.

                    7 August 1958

THE MAGIC

The magic only stays
As long as stars are shining
As long as there's a summer moon
In silver clouds reclining;

As long as summer answers
When lonely breezes sigh
And sing each loving day to sleep
With summer lullabye

(And we who knew magic
And love without name
May block out the memory
But ne'er be the same.)

And magic only stays
As long as stars are bright
But there always will be stars
In every summer night.

29 August 1958

THE FEW

The few have come
    who know the stars
They lead, who stay alive,
As severed masses
    bleed and sigh
And silver half-clouds
    sleep to die.

September 1958

COMMUNE

Why is it that little trees huddle together?
They all look alike and they huddle together, together.

A lone little tree could be just as a feather
In wind and high weather, high weather, high weather
Lest the tap root be deep where it fastens the feather,
Fastens the feather, the feather, the feather.

There is sunlight to grow in alone on the heather
There is time to rejoice when you've conquered the heather,
                            the heather, the heather.

Why is it that little trees live all together?
Their branches entangle and die close together, together
They lean different ways, but the roots are together
They all look alike and they die on the heather.

And they die close together, together, together
Together. . . . .

                        1 December 1958

ADONIS

Blue as his eyes are the heavens
For nothing could be bluer than his eyes
Blue as his eyes are the waters
The sea is but a mirror to the skies

Slender as his stance is the willow
For nothing could be suppler than his frame
Straight as his body is the oak tree
It's beauty was created in his name.

Deathless as his spirit is Time's wisdom
For nothing could embrace more than his soul
Noble and as gentle as his living
A world in parts has now become a whole.

12 December 1958

RECOGNITION

Tall darkness of youth
Strength to my heart and mind
Conquer what must succomb to you
Know and love what conquers you

What sleeps in shadows
Waiting for your light of truth
Valiently and prince-like seek the forms
That only need your touch to live.

12 December 1958

PROVIDENCE

Through the hush of memories yet to come
I hear the voice of one who knows me
Speaking gently, wisely to my loneliness
Part of me speaking to me
I only met him yesterday and knew
He was tomorrow

I must go on alone
So must he
The half-remembered future
Searching frantically the past
To learn what has been taught
While we were asleep.

This alone binds us
The apartness makes a unity
Nature's way holds forever
The joys of waking days in
Hands too strong to drop a precious gift
And strengthless to crush it.

I would like to play with Fate
Gamble
I would like to play as others do
Providence would have me to herself now
I am figured in with different plans
And cannot veer
Even to play awhile
Make tea from rainwater
And not pay with my heart

By fortune the heart forgets
What is of the heart alone

The heart cannot forget
The tremblings of the soul--
Senseless to the quaking of another world
What awakes in both heart and mind
Cannot be put to bed
By one alone
Only leave as it came.

17 December 1958

Transmit True and Brightly

I must have wind
Race with it and lose
I must have rain
Laugh with it and die
I must have storm
Fight with it and Be

                    17 December 1958

TRANSITION

A city in shadow. . .
The grayness of slumber
Spread itself o'er dreaming buildings.

Unperturbed,
A single ray of light
Found a path
Through changing clouds
And gently woke each drowsy brick.

Then from spires and towers
It fell upon my face;
And as I wondered whence the warmth
I looked up and saw the Source.

. . .A city in sunlight!

8 January 1959

Takes time

Takes time for a scar to heal

Till the traces disappear

The inside is alive and renews itself

But a wound leaves a mark

On the dead epidermis

Oh it will go away

But it takes time

8 January 1959

A city in shadow –

The gray blanket of slumber

Spreads itself o'er dreaming buildings.

Unperturbed,

A single ray of light

Found a pathway

Through the maze of clouds

And gently woke each drowsy brick.

Then from between skyscrapers

It fell upon my face;

And as I wondered whence the warmth

I looked up and saw the source,

A city in sunlight.

Dreams are for children

And fairy tales

Only a magic sword

Can conquer the forest

Enchanted woods

Wielded by a prince true hearted

And brave.

A prince of heart, not blood

Waited for a hundred years

Patience, patience

A century she loved the same

A century hence she will remain

The princess' spirit

A gardener's daughter

A dream flickered before her eyes

Behind her eyes

She slept

Patience, Patience

Oh to wake, to live on earth

A hundred years to wait

Perhaps a hundred more

A realm above

A prince came through with magic sword
Patience, patience held his hand
He lived on earth a hundred years
Perhaps a hundred more to go

A realm below

By heavenly word from earthly mouth
And human kiss returned from time
A hundred years is much too short
A hundred years is just a day

Dreams, enchantment, magic sword
A gardener's daughter and her lord
For children, yes,
A hundred years is just a day.

13 January 1959

Transmit True and Brightly

ORNAMENTS

Wonder steals away
When knowledge enters in
Angels hang on walls

Sunrise rose pinkness purity
Glass-like clear
The first step breaks the mirror
And ripples spring from one small foot
Gone the burning morning clouds
Specks of flame
Bridge the peaks from swell to swell

Wonder gently leaves
When knowledge steals in
Angels hang on walls.

25 January 1959

A GLIMPSE

A glimpse of what can be
And then to turn away?
To fail is not to die.
To win is not to live
Risks and patience
A couple suited
Creations sure to live
Created but to live
Created to create.
A life born
The life earned
God was not created.
A flicker of God, a soul--
Perhaps an hour. . .
Beyond creation then
An hour
A day
Even half an hour
Even half a flicker
Created to create
Not perform.
All trust be in sustainment
All trust be in a Friend.

                        9 February 1959

CHICAGO

Tribal haunts of many moons
Ceremonial sacrifice
Bricks surround the campfire smoke
Iron hovers o'er the coals

Steel teepees line the plains
Sidewalks path the marshy floor
Wild onions fight to stand
Lake flows into river.

                    20 February 1959

My heart was high within me,
I wondered at the blue;
The slanting gold of April
Had quickly dried the dew.

Up sprang the wind of morning
From prairies freshly plowed
And fragrance from the topsoil
Perfumed each gilded cloud.

Then off they traveled seaward--
My heart would with them fly
O'er valley, desert, mountain--
The clouds know where to die.

But I am in my city
My plains are young as spring
Before I seek my silence
I first must learn to sing.

My faith is in these green buds;
My hope is in the sky;
I love this ground. And mountains
Will wait 'til time to die.

1 April 1959

To R.F.L.G.

I shall give you the light in my heart
That you'll see in the star-forlorn night
I shall give you the joy on my lips
So that beauty will sing through your sight.

I shall give you the spark of my mind
It will add to the flame in your own
I shall give you the hope of my hand
So your mountain is not cold and lone.

I shall give you the truth of my soul
That you'll stand in the fall of the earth
I shall give you my faith and my love
And star-shine will cry a new birth.

20 April 1959

MILES WAIT

Miles wait 'til set of sun;
Hours fly through stone and wood;
As if man saw when first he stood
His first short steps that need be won.

Fortune's burden gravitates;
The sword of sorrow cleans the heart;
And all negations do impart
The challenge Nature radiates.

1 June 1959

CHOSEN

The stars knew him and were glad
He held the planets in his hand
And the moon on his brow
Shadows warmed him
And he won the night to his arms
Then blackness moved up and away
Purple clouds gave way to gold
And he observed
Night wind cried and echoed in his soul
While sunbeams danced lightly there
Bounding from the outer shell.

As he grieved an eagle call
Carried him to lofty ice
And brilliant hues that heeded Time
Provided ways, provided peaks
Pines spoke softly at the height
In the forest night in day
He learned from them and from the streams
And weaned himself on Man.

18 August 1959

AT EDGEWOOD

Oh the coming and the going
In the yellow sky of living
And the green and brown of sleep

Oh the knowing and the loving
In the orange clouds of dreaming
And the red and gray of Time

Oh the parting and returning
In the purple wind of Being
And the blue and white of God

29 August 1959

M^cKEE

Love the brave hello
That shakes the grassy rock,
That vibrates from the hillside
In solitary song.

Whisk away the night
That seeps into the springtime,
That grows upon the morning
With shadow seeking step.

Mourn the dying cry
Which holds the living earth
And sucks the river waters
To liquify the dirge.

Whisper to the sun
That stays the rush of evening,
That burns the ice in winter
With triumphant shout.

12 October 1959

CYCLE

Breaking barely grass design
Of autumn fields with sprightly tread,
An old man stark as wintered pine
Did not believe the grain was dead.

In retrospect he sighted Spring
And lingered on the cherry blush
When no blue dome defied the wing
And no chant stayed the wind-song rush.

A rooted seedling felt the sun.
The first green blade was drawn through brown;
A young man waited free to run
And vie the hills for Summer's crown.

Earth supported sturdy leaf,
Knee-high when bombs brought even bright;
Sky quenched thirst in misty grief,
Star food held the gift of night.

A man beheld in memory mind
The harvest and the gold appear
When fall rays entered him to find
A place hushed, still full ripened clear.

Peace cadencing threshing came
Upon an old man as soft snow
Flew swift o'er barley grass and flame
Of leaves that waking green would show.

                    6 November 1959

SUDDEN REMEMBERING

A golden streak unites two clouds
At ev'ning brightened west;
From far away and long ago
Those souls shall never rest.

Duty chains the lovely morn,
Mystery binds across the night
Lovers fading fast from day
At sunset linked in purple light.

Moonset gives the pure white ash
That sunfire pleads for all the day;
And when that flame flies o'er the hills,
We'll be one in every way.

8 January 1960

LEAVE

Leave me stay in beauty
And wonder after love
Must I do a duty
I know nothing of?

I shall wait for dying,
Stilled before my youth,
If I can't be flying
With the winds of truth.

Will you know my longing,
Comprēhend my grief?
Who would I be wronging
If my life were brief?

                    1 March 1960

TO THE SPIRIT OF TALIESIN

You listened while I tried to speak
When I returned the desert way;
And first my heart was fainting weak
From seeing part of yesterday.

You and only you I told
How I estranged myself from peace,
How my soul walked lone and cold,
And how my natural joy did cease.

As I spoke, I felt within
A ray of hopefullness appear;
And what I thought was discipline
Became the freedom from my fear.

In you is all I ever knew--
But just beyond my younger sight.
My own true spirits there in you
And what could be my source of light.   21 March 1960

TO OLEY

To love and love completely,
To give and smile so sweetly. . .
Pardon my innocence---
Such are the thoughts of a youngster.
Pardon my beauty,
That is my way.

I knew and you
Knew me.
Magic ---as it were---
The wind of the sea
Speaking.
All I had to give,
All that I could love
In vain.

I'm a fool,
But being a fool, leave me go my way
And learn.
The sea teaches, does it not?
Man teaches, but not beauty,
Not me.
Only scratches skin sunburned from nature---
Raw.
But healthy.

Sticks and stone may
Break my bones but
Poems never hurt me.

1 April 1960

Southern

California

Transmit True and Brightly

VENICE WEST

Changing shades and forms. . .
What are you with children
Across my blurry rooms of candles?

If you were mine
Would I know you yet in love?
And still at one with me,
Only light that once bridged night
Could ever hope as you
Shouted hope in one soft glance.

What is the form of love you are?
Are you near my longing,
On your way,
Or in the Northlands yet—
Where is the shadow of your soul?

Or can it be that once—
And then forever
Here?

                                        11 April, 1960

David

Thank God for your eyes

That young from pain

Were purer than my own

And called me to the sand

You hunched and ragged drunkard

Who knew the torment

More than youth which

Fighting for my heart

Won

For a while

"don't dream – do!"

Oh mystic force that used your face

Freed and lightened

All my days and mornings

Even nights are sweeter now

As I return

And you drift off again.

David...

Thank God.

April 11, 1960

THE GIFT

Tender grey as the night you came,
A gentle heart in touch with mine,
And soon from mystery leaped a flame
That sighed to be that certain sign.

My green soul longs to rest in yours
And gaze into your placid deeps;
But joy! How blue the ocean roars;
How yon glad misty mountain weeps!

Free wind rustles silent sand;
Could you give me liberty?
Desert moonlight knows my hand;
Would you be a part of me?

13 April 1960

TO SOMEONE WHO KNOWS ME

Wax rose and lightened,
Your maker made you warm to melt
And glow inside.
Waxy leaf he cut and
Fused in love beneath white petals.
To time your life has burned my thumb
And I am glad of pain for beauty
Wax rose--your core sinks deeper;
And faintly seen is light that once could
Singe a bee.
And stupid people break your leaf
Which grew cold watching for
A light from other worlds.

Come back, maker!
Bring your gentle flame
And soften,
Reshape leaf and petal.

Wax rose--
Don't die before your candle soul
Is found and fired
Under tender hands
And quiet heart
Creating you in wonder,
Returning now in silence.

                    21 April 1960

Transmit True and Brightly

THAT IS THE QUESTION

Two thousand miles
To wake and know the love--
Continental edge and high divide
Prodded sleepy soul.

Ah me! How simple just
To stay for pity's sake.
Why live if someone else will die?
But now the sea in all eternal wisdom
Lives
While fish and bird
And ship and plane
Give the surface blue and
Sink to death beneath.

And lava lives inside new hills
And lava kills
What touches boiling ore
When it bursts its bands of clay,
When it goes free.

Why die if life is strong?
Why die at all?. . .
Unless to live in static sea
Or rushing rock.

                                29 April 1960

CRYSTAL COVE

Slender palms swayed lightly on the sand
And shore birds sang in haunting harmony
Under mystic skies of opal clouds
The hills far off were bending to the sea.

I leaped gaily to the waiting song
And swam my heart out in the tidal foam
In solitude beneath a salty sun
I stood and heard the wind say I was home.

Then off to bamboo hut I gently ran
Delighted by the pebbles on the way
And glad was I to hear the ocean crash
Beneath the moon, recalling each today.

21 May 1960

LIGHTED

So dimly lit
Through months of sea and palms,
The college where I walked
Deep in my work,
And where I ran down creaky
Dormitory stairs
To wait for rain to end
And snow to fly.
So soft it seemed in Spring light.
And evening glowed right
Through the golden pane.
Room-mate laughing--
Dress for Prom--
And when I saw the school in Autumn
All booky, red and gold,
And pine smoke ran
Suspending words along a page,
Recalling green ravines
In May
And lilacs where we climbed among
The graves
I loved

31 May 1960

IN VENICE

Dusky red and
Pearled in the morning,
I with you
Felt wings flit by
And wished that lightness
To our own
Heavy ribs.
Miles would speed
And hours knew we were
But never shall be
Dusky again,
Pearled by the sea
And wishing for white wings.

                              6 June 1960

LET ME NEVER

Leave me in sorrow
That knows no morrow
Am I a fool for Liberty?

Each one beside me
Offers to guide me.
May I alone know
Harmony?

So take me fast away--
Oh let me never say,
"I will be free!"

6 June 1960

ALONE

I am one solitary stalk
Who needs her field of earth.
My head is growing ripe too soon
And salty from this air.
I have known the beauty of the ocean day
And now return to grassland
Before the harvest moon;
For who would gather up
A single grain
And growing wild?

                    21 June 1960

SOJOURN

Wheat of windy plains and green,
The short-clipped lawns,
Oaks strong in rain
And begging to be held. . .

I stole away when evening died,
Searched out the blaze,
And found
That it slept
Just behind the sea.

21 June 1960

To go in verdant solitude

And spend a golden day

With heaving chest and pounding breast

O'er mounting hills of May

And dark-shoed dells beneath me

The towering hills between

And you were there

To hold a hand that wasn't

Eyes sparkling in the air

To sit on a log beside you

And see your wind-tossed hair

To have a heart of thunder

And sense among the green

That you were there

To hold the cup of ecstasy

And drink from the very top

To take to satiation

And not to lack a drop

To laugh with unseen pleasure

And shout it to the sky

Feel a solitary presence

And know with certain knowledge

And not to have to dream

That you were there

To live in pensive solitude

And spend a quiet day

And tear-filled eyes – a soft surprise

Recalling hills of May

The dark-shoed dells remembered

Through misty memory seen

And you were there.

Illinois - June

Wheat, of windy plains
And green,
The short-clipped lawns,
Oaks, strong in rain
And begging to be held.

I stole away when
    evening died,
Searched out the blaze,
And found
That it slept
Just behind the sea.

6-21-60
Nancy Summ

Illinois

Wheat of windy plains
And green,
The short-clipped lawns,
Oaks, strong in rain
And beginning to be held.

I stole away when evening died,
Searched out the blaze,
And found
That it slept
Just behind the sea.

21 June 1960

IN THE FALL

One man's arms will hold me in the Fall
And I'll love him true and tenderly.
Once behind the sacred wedding wall,
One vow shall unveil eternity.

Soon the glimmering girl will die away,
Embraced in Summer's ardent afterglow;
And I shall be a woman, glad to stay
Beside one man, the only love I know.

Be warned young lads and lovers wanting me
Kindle not those embers into fire!
For I've such a short while to be free
That you'll be scorched and calling me a liar.

29 June 1960

<u>SESTINA</u>

I

I have seen the virgin April cloud
Dancing, drifting out across the blue,
Lingering on the desert,
Wondering for her brother,
Finding gentle lover,
Hoping winds were true.

II

Winds change, but the sky is always true;
And so--was blown away the April cloud,
Losing sight of lover
In the springtime blue,
Left behind her brother
Wondering the desert.

III

Never quite forgotten was the desert,
    (the sky was in the cloud and kept her true,)
Asking for her brother--
Would he love a cloud?
And the April blue
Lingered in her lover.

IV

Weeping in the star-light was her lover
Thinking that the magic left the desert
And his eyes were blue.
April skies are true.
And the gentle cloud
Wondered for her brother.

V

Patient still and wondering was her brother,
Watching springtime heavens for the cloud.
And her April lover
Left the gentle desert.
So, as wind is true,
Shifted eyes of blue.

VI

Fierce and piercing was the loss of blue
And so the cloud went weeping for her brother.
He was always true,
Wishing to be lover
In the springtime desert
To the April cloud.

1 July, 1960

- 79 -

The Twins

Divided heart!

My soul is two in love

Shall forever be

Along the shore

And wand'ring in the hills,

Or resting on the plains/

Will love be light or dark

Artist, scholar?

(Perhaps, I'll seek the desert

Between the prairie and the sea,

Where spirits ride

On wind that's free

From soot and salt,

And love my unknown brother)

My God, my God!

I beg of You to tell me!

Speak in peaceful sea,

Or show me fertile soil.

(Whisper through my

Shifting sister,

Sand.)

11 July 1960

THE TWINS

Divided heart--
My soul is two in love.
Shall forever be
Along the shore
And wand'ring in the hills
Or resting on the plains?
Light or dark?
Artist? Scholar?

Perhaps I'll seek the desert,
Between the prairie and the sea
Where spirits ride on wind that's free
Of salt and soot. . .
And love my unknown brother.
If God exists, I beg of Him
To tell me,
Speak in peaceful sea
Or show me fertile soil;
Whisper through
My shifting sister
Sand.

11 July, 1960

TO A HESITANT YOUNG MAN

Let love come
But do not tarry--
Prairies also call the soul.
Do not be afraid to carry
Beauty, lest it ask a toll.

Take love now
Or ever wander
Through the cliffs beside the sea;
A rose can't give
Herself--though fonder
Grows her silent love for thee.

14 July, 1960

IN HEARING BRAHMS VIOLIN CONCERTO

An unknown sigh lies deep within my breast,
The violin to draw it out in tears;
And echoes of that grief
Wait in darkest corners.
Vision blurs in blue and flame
As old salt pain
Knows my cheek and wondering eye.

What can there be so far away and true
That calls to me?
What is there in the heart's deep care
That reaches down to me
And pleads with me
To see.   31 July, 1960

I SHALL SEE

I have seen that dream before:
To fix my course in time
Parallel to yours,
And finishing our climb,
Turn to you at last
And stand beside you then,
Knowing all has passed;
I shall see that dream again.

August, 1960

HAPPY GOD

Ho-tai lies exhausted
Beneath the modern masterwork.
Growing pains are sharper when
Ecstasy is shed for peace.

Ho-tai lies exhausted
And slightly disappointed in
A certain masterwork
Which hangs serenly on the
Wall above.

10 September, 1960

Reminiscence

I have known that dream before –

To fix my course in time

Parallel to yours

And finishing our climb

Turn to you at last

And stand beside you then

Knowing all has passed

I shall see that dream again.

September 14, 1960

NEW YEAR'S EVE

Wring out the old
Tears and heart-shreds;
At midnight this year will not exist.
It's good to be refreshed
In the birth of next time,
But all new days
Are tinted by the past
Despite the fact that
Yesterday does not exist.

In this new phase of time
Lilac trees may not bloom,
Orange groves may not bring forth.
There is a soul waiting
To make an entrance, even if
There are no potatoes.
This year does not exist, tomorrow.

Let old acquaintence be forgot
And for a tiny gold
Ring in the new!

31 December, 1960

A FAREWELL

My dear, these golden days will fly:
And with the years
Our dreaming alters course.

Tho' through some lovely act of God
Our souls continue one,
Remember that embrace,
That long last look
When beating hearts and love
Locked in the now and ever.
(And oh, how warm it was!)

Spring-spoken hope
Still whispers in my soul;
Your waiting arms
Will keep the snow-lost rose.

28 January, 1961

SOMEWHERE

Softly dim as even shade
Jasmine and the moon appear;
Slow above the fragrant glade
Capricorn begins a year.

Palms bedeck my chosen home,
Undying spring walks lone with me;
Sunny sand and salty foam
Now comprise my destiny.

Once I had a prairie heart--
Still my prayers are Northland bound,
Longing, dreaming to depart,
Escape the crashing tidal sound.

Yet the fates entreat me stay;
I cannot hush their silent call.
Somewhere I gave my life away
Between the sea and mountain wall.

                    10 February, 1961

ALPHA

Through a scarlet screaming night
Gemini shone silent
In the first hours of the sign.

Mercury soared to tell the sky
Of life so early torn from dark
Deep in the womb.

Then breath—soft gasping cry—
Man child met the dawn.

26 May, 1961

ECLIPSE

Eclipse -- the secret of the sky!
Planet shadow falls
Across a rock-back mirror moon,
Completing black out there.

Still a silver bow drawn down
And then
We cannot see the arrows in their flight
Or know their destination.

25 August, 1961

AND BEING YOUNG

Oh fragile word, escape me not.
Sweet image, stay within my sight!
So darkling, I, without the twain
Yet being near to light.

I live to learn from birds a-wind,
I wax and wane in Plato's night.
If ink or page deny my hand
I still know one plume bright.

I've lost my heart to handsome Earth
And dying, I shall fiercely fight
For Beauty (Fly to me and sing!)
And Truth the learned light.

                              25 August, 1961

FROM SEPTEMBER

The honor lies in knowing you forever
Your tenderness in Kissing me good-bye,
Your strength composed in every heart of oak.
Forsake the earth, and I soon hence shall fly.
You cannot leave the soul that's part of you.
You cannot leave me desolate to mourn---
Let me go first; come bend above my death bed
And hold me 'til there is no more to hold.
Until you hear me singing, calling through,
Kiss my still eyes, the once bright hair still stroke;
Then gently sleep that we may be reborn.
There must be trails that we serenely tread.
In time ahead the path ways shall not sever
But wind into the prairie Autumn gold.

7 September, 1961

DIMENSION

What bright and bursting prisms play
Upon sweet stolen hours –
Free youth lay trembling on my thigh
Unafraid as light.

Strange spectrum of unearthly powers,
Sanctuary find a night
When sprites inhabit fertile clay
Unafraid as I.

26 October 1961

THE KNOWING

The knowing comes along a private pain
And through these fingers scribbling tired
As for a time and ever
I am alone with me.

Still fearing chains
Yet fond and hesitant to run
The wild heart stirs the halting hand
And quickens starfire tread.

I am the instrument--
Moon-blown seas,
Snow clouded peaks,
And of my far wind self.

                          9 March, 1962

SOUL DRAWN OUT

Soul drawn out and shattered
Far from the plains that mothered me,
Tortured at the warm shell hand,
Bruised and bitten--bitches yap,
The beautiful too frail for them.

What truth can win the still-eyed?
Better sing and never try at all!

23 May, 1962

A TRIBUTE TO MY BIRTHPLACE

Kingliest of all the manly towns,

Blue diadem upon an earthen heart,

I shout to you from in a woman's gown

And love you for your life more than your art.

(And yet I've known great beauty in your

Spires between the mists and vernal rain;

And once on August shores of mulberry bough

Caught me and the water broke again)

A Neon scepter blazes the plains

And prairies yield ripe treasure to the call,

Until at last a dying sun remains

At rest beyond the royal harvest wall.

24 July 1962

OUT OF THE WIND

Out of the wind that darkens me
Draw this wild heart
And lead about the strings of time
Herd not the heavy bells of blue
October
Ringing how the chimes of Summer
Float and beautifully sing and fade
But dance the frightening gyre
Of love accessable but unfulfilled
Eternally until this span of days
This chance of many lives.

                              18 October, 1962

TO THE MOON

Your deep sea aura is

The earth

As seen from this swift orbit

Swinging near your flaming

Morning mate

And my own racing light

Touches a dark side softly as

I pass

My natural ever circling course

May wound a wasting world

To meet the ruddy sun

And blast a bunch of space.

23 October 1962

FOR KARL

One journey last
Conceived in wind and flame
To sail a soul to realms
Where love
Can call a sunbeam to the heart.

If from the ancient rigging
Breath were taken blue
Never to know another earthly form
I now would sleep in joy
For I have tasted salt upon
The bow and in
The wildest light.

                              23 October, 1962

NEARLY

You can go now
Forget and
We are no longer bound
The traces disappeared at dawn
Gone
Lost in a quivering clot
Untamed again
Go back now
Maybe next time
You'll saya
Maybe next
Time

13 November, 1962

TO WHOM IT MAY CONCERN

The things of beauty
Kindle only pain in
Kindling
Dried and dying men
And pain where pain is wanted
Needed for the gossip smoke
Small green fires
Growing

20 November, 1962

THE HAND THAT RULES

The hand that rules the bitter
Christmas spring
Formed this, my youth.
And I repent of wanting
Nature in the sun
The blue night through,
The willing flight across soft
Meadows to the morn,
The dells of solitude from which
I shouted to the earth.
Long snow blown hours must close
Before the world is young again. . .
Unageing longing.

2 December, 1962

SIMILE

When I perceive the jealous river ice
Close binding, bank to bank, an anxious stream
Wild spurting currents from the heart I see
Chilled silent in the loud snare of the brain.

I know that guardian of the unborn grain--
The crystal death--sleep that inhibits spring--
Is kin to intellect, a glittering quilt,
Treacherous patchwork blanketing the ghost.

From Winter in the power of the frost,
Skull polishers, great grinding glaciers move,
Slow promising a thaw that never can
Release a brooklet after love is numb.

25 January, 1963

LIKE, MAN!

Baby, babe,
I dig that tender heart
Above my own
Fast beating in the night
Or just before a mellow dawn.
The wrinkled sheets that held us
Warm and tough with love
Lost all the cool to come
Getting fixed.
I dig your tough soul, Baby.

                    6 February, 1963

Transmit True and Brightly

A LITTLE LIFE

A LITTLE LIFE CAME LABOURING
       FROM MY THIGHS
AND CRIED A TENDER SPIRIT BACK
       TO EARTH
THE TINY FOLDED FISTS, THE
       BRIGHTENING EYES,
A LITTLE GIRL OF LIFE,
       A HAPPY BIRTH.

21 September, 1963

Transmit True and Brightly

NARCISSUS

Wild freedom such as men
    but seldom know,
Sweet venture on the humming
    of a heart,
Discovering and distributing
    to men,
The holy secrets that reveal
    great inward power.
Defraud the spirit in its
    sacred search
Vainly calling virtue
    and to fame.

19 October, 1963

Transmit True and Brightly

RISING IN THE EAST

A cross stood in the steepening star
That slung a sleepy stable to the sword,
And startled solitary sheep
Sang before the stone.

A star beat in the infant heart,
The rays upraising, praising in the night
Beneath his breastbone lower blood
Bleating beaten lamb

A heart shines in the secret tree.
Lovely tree that rustles in the stars
And all the prancing rams, all wandering wolves
Listen to the laughter of those limbs.

Where lights eternal, temporary cross.

15 November, 1963
Revised 18 December, 1969

MY LOVE LIVES

My love lives all around myself;
Above and in the starry forms
That ruled the sweet first meeting.
And in clear blue and every
Wind or storm that finds me;

And when I pick a pebble from the sea,
Stoop to breathe that perfume of the earth,
My love lives underneath my step;
He is the worn rug where my children creep
By day--and when I lullabye the little ones,
My love lies just beneath the tune;

My love lives right beside myself--
I reach to light the lamp, to fill the cup,
Or gaze straight out to dawn--
My love is in the morning cool gold air
Beside the sun and me;

Behind me lives my love in
Younger days, the past composed
Of moments great and mean,
And my love lives ahead of me unknown
At points in time I neither love nor fear.

My love lives all around myself
And in.

                          21 June, 1964

TO MY SWEET

To art, the frosting on the cake
Of life I eat
My teeth devour the dark
Bread loaf
And after nourishment comes cake
But what craves frosting?
The dreamer in us all?
That fine uplifting force that
Raises cultures from the caves?
Not these, it is
A demon truth
A parasite called beauty.
For what decays more sweetly,
Painlessly,
Than frosting?

9 September, 1964

THREE QUESTIONS FROM THE CLOUDS

Caring, will the care

Begin to cloy the current and

The candor of winged girls

Of thunder vested boys?

Could it be union at the fall

Perception through a certain

Veiled pain

A struggling Leda

At the great swan's loin?

Or shall we merely open our valises

Display and pack away again unchanged

Our secret curios and feathered souvenirs;

Conceiving in a single singing thrust

Bitter wistful laughter

In the after?   *26 September 1964*

United pulse, oh flee the common beating
Hearts; love's greatest joy may bring the
                    greatest pain.
And when we touch, deny the inner meeting
Forces--tasting truth may snare a wary brain,
Enslaving; for to love provides no place
                    but near you,
Beside you, or behind your quickening heels--
And you choose where, Thereby is born the fear to
Draw so close that deepening light reveals.

                    5 January, 1965

HEARTS AND TRUFFLES

Fickle as the moon in sending
Lovers to a dream of light,
Beauty bears the laugh of lending
Wings to darkling, parting flight.

When the leaves grieve for giving
Pearls and tears the mind rejects,
Knows that love is for the living,
Dreams are light the moon reflects.

14 February 1965

FLAMENCO

Distantly castanets
Six-stringed pilgrimage
Time is a shy guitar.

Flashing assymetry
Gypsy geometry
Love is a wild guitar.

Minaret melody
Singly and mournfully
Life is a lone guitar.

14 January, 1966

AFTER A GRAVE

My every pulse, whose beating
Proved I lived,
With death-like voids
Alternated
Til void alone remained;
The thudding ceased while still
You were a boy,

From this new day,
Beneath this fresh gold
On my skull,
I wonder at your whitening form
And your slow heart.

Remember when you
Loved me for my eyes?

May, 1966

Chicagoland

A world of loving in his deep eye
Shy rhythm swinging out along his
Subtle singing step
Mere gesture draws delicious
Warm and living liquor
From a startled heart and
Then to touching
Taste completely sweet
Intoxication.

August, 1966

Until the song of the world is found
Man may not marry his muse undead;
Living hearts hold to the mortal dream.

Winning and healing the human wound
Spirits of love have sighed and bled
For lovers to lie in the starry scheme.

Will no living man forsake the sound
Of fleeting applause for an astral bed
Breathe on the breast 6f a secret scream?

24 August, 1966

I come to live
To love or bury love
To never ask but hold
A word, a brightening glance
Unspoken dream
And silence sometimes is
The dearest gift.

November, 1966

WINTER HOUSE

A ready den so heated
That the weather spins
Free flakes to window stain--
Wet sectored pane--
Come crystaling down the frost.

The same sun summer shines
Into my winter house
But now the light is blue and waiting
Gold to complement.

2 December, 1966

Nothing has changed
Winter still is drifting from the skies,
Few songs still stand around me;
The music often flows into your hand
And your still hesitating pluck
On yielding strings.
Release the sanquine surge
That lies beneath the strum
Before it sleeps to dream.
Few songs stand still around me
Still as winter raging from the skies
Changed is nothing.

                          10 February, 1967

Devout as water to water
A current on the sea bed stirs
I move beneath the surface tides
We are the same
You lash the land and carry all
creation on your waves
I do not touch the shore
Perhaps we never shall be
Still together
Laugh
We are the same

30 June, 1967

What life between the tropics swells?
Sun Stars so sweetly heat
Increasing beat
The belly of the earth on primal ooze
Together steaming
Complement.

Beyond the tropic lattitudes
Outside
Stands written history and the mad wars
Search and hope for love but let it go
Shutting doors sad
Goodbyes for nothing
Cool and colder to the poles alone
And opposite.

So let us turn our journey in
To fly in awe as space between us dies,
And fuse.

                    July, 1967

<u>1967</u>

This year has raged
And dreamed
And dropped its music on
Fierce summer
In the umbre
Of the Earth.

Storming free the elements
To snow the people in
Their pride.
The wind so huge
And hollow funnel
Gusts that broke and bled
This nature year of change.

Unleashed, unswerved by all sciences,
This year has screamed the gyre
And sung
The moon descending to
Wild slumber
In the umbre
Of the Earth.

August, 1967

THUG JOE

Hello?
Yes, this is Thug Joe.
Lunch and Buckingham afternoon?
I'm stunned
Are you sure?
This is Thug Joe
You know.
I'm terrible at madrigals
And all my dough is tied up in trust.
I can't send you to Puerto Rico
Or Rome.
Why me?
And my character is only sterling
Plate.
Why me?
Are you sure?
Why Thug Joe?

October, 1967

INCANTATION

Fragile touch me
Look to Earth
Water and water seeking fire
Wands may murmur
Breathe and fly
Mother all my blood is air
Coins before me
Air will change
Earth bound water
Mud or cups
Running over
Look within
Water to water
Flowing fire.

                    29 November, 1967

Rest the lover in your smile
Turn your eyes from me.
Let love sleep a little while
Just to keep it free
Make your music ___ play your part ⏤
meander merrily
And when you tire, trust my heart ─
Turn your eyes to me.

                    6 December, 1967

Space and swift blue after
Love and all its
Royal fire
You are and
Love is
Home blue so swift
We dare the deity
To space.

                              28 January, 1968

Never return to today
We are
All love is
Come catch me soft
And strong as
Forever
Gone in a whisper of now.

25 January, 1968

Tender grey as night you came
A gentle soul in touch with mine
And soon from mystery leaped a flame
That sighed to be that certain sign.

My song longs to rest in yours
And sink into your darking deeps
BUT JOY! How blue the ocean roars
How you glad misty mountain weeps.

When every girl's a firebrand
Could you be a part of me?
Gypsy music knows my hand
Do you want the heart of me?

                    18 July, 1968

A PRETTY CRAB IS LIKE AN EXERCISE

The music we have spun
Spins on. The song is done.
We stop the silver threaded strum
From sounding on the ether hum
Retreat from love to separate silent shells
Poke out a claw
(Perhaps the rhythm beaten shore)
It came too close
That tune
It nearly sang us to the sea
No more
That silver threaded song
Is gone
The music we have spun
Spins on. The song is done.

7 November, 1968

And pine smoke ran

Suspending words along a page

Recalling green ravines

In May

And lilacs where we climbed

I loved

And now my love has come to me

In other form

Beside the tide

But I am sad at heart

For loving lost the plains

So strangely lit

In future mystery

I threw our fist born

Long awaited child

Into the cold woods alone

Because I wanted him

To learn life fast

Survive and love

But the hungry birds came

And pecked his eyes away

And a fox tore his tiny heart

The precious one, the child,

Love long awaited

Comes only once

And I threw it into the forest alone

The night I found you

Helpless with lust

Invited the serpent

And ran.

9 December 1968

RISING IN THE EAST

A cross stood in the steepening star
That slung a sleepy stable to the sword,
And startled solitary sheep
Sang before the stone.

A star beat in the infant heart,
The rays upraising, praising in the night
Beneath his breastbone lower blood
Bleating beaten lamb

A heart shines in the secret tree.
Lovely tree that rustles in the stars
And all the prancing rams, all wandering wolves
Listen to the laughter of those limbs.

Where lights eternal, temporary cross.

15 November, 1963
Revised 18 December, 1969

WHO IS NUMBER TWO

Thrust and grieve, Chicago,
Now laugh it all away
Constitutional storm center
Crazed heretic,
You have rocked our heritage
On your hot lap
And knocked away the masks!
Wheezing, aching, stinking,
The national poisons drain out in
The sauna of your sweat.
Work and moan again, Chicago,
Laugh it all away.

2 October, 1970

Mad-City

At my (and final) dark
Sweet hour
The specks of gold congeal to
Form a face of yours
Your only face.

The one that turns to me
So sweet the hour
When gold specks run
To silhouette--to full--

16 January, 1973

Newest now of all the

Summers lost

Cries great against

Beginning Northern sun

Dark frozen lawns resist

Come melting sweet for

Running of the frost.

I ride my spectacle alive

On fruit that ripens shining

Or rots lost.

1 February 1973

BRIGHT SUNNY DAYS
Like streamers run
Explosive and gone fast
Before the eyes of those
Who watch.
I see the trails of dying smoke
Caught in the evening
Wind and come apart
Like atoms
Like a soul.

                              11 February, 1973

Diocletian Palace

And the whole trip

Rests

Adriatic sunset

On the old world

Breasts

Starigrad and wading

Lavender and shading

Sheepskin, tiles, and Hvar

Remember Hvar.

3 March 1973

I am one solitary stalk

Who needs her field of earth

My head is growing ripe too soon

And salty from this air.

Oh – I could choose a mountain

And die perhaps between the rocks

The sand will not nourish –

Neither the sea, for I cannot

Pretend to be a palm

On shore with seaweed.

I have known the beauty of this ocean day

And shall return to grasslands

Before the harvest moon

For who would gather up

One single grain of wheat

Growing wild?

You all did love him once

Without cause

What cause withholds you,

Then, to move on for him?

O judgement! Thou art fled

To brutish beasts,

And men <who> lost their reason

Two winds had I beside my heart

And wondered which

Would find a resting place therein

North wind and flame and brown

Sent homey scents of autumn plains

So lonely in their waiting

For the northern snow

And every cruel April

Promised then gave way to maple smoke

And big oak deaths

Made known hungry

North wind sighs

Blue and yellow West Sea Wind

Walked around the mountains

Lonely as a star

Restless on the silent desert

And shy to look at me

Or give me warmth

So I reached out with my heart

And the blue and yellow beige

Came and swept a while

Warming me forever

While young north wind howls still

Upon the prairie ice

And rustles April elms

What life between the tropics swells?

Sun – starts – so sweetly heat –

Increasing beat –

The belly of the earth on primal ooze

Together steaming

Complement.

Beyond the tropic latitudes

Outside

Stands written history and the mad wars

Search and hope for love but let it go

Shutting doors   sad

Goodbyes for nothing

Cool and colder to the poles

Alone

And opposite

So let us turn our journey IN

To fly in awe as space between us dies

AND FUSE.

19 July 1974 NR (Nancy Roderick)

What life between the tropics swells?
Sun — stars - so sweetly heat -
Increasing beat -
The belly of the earth on primal ooze
Together steaming
Complement.

Beyond the tropic lattitudes
Outside
Stands written history and the mad wars
Search and hope for love but let it go
Shutting doors   sad
Goodbyes   for   nothing
Cool and colder to the poles
Alone
And opposite

So let us turn our journey IN
To fly in awe as space between us dies
AND FUSE.

19 July 1974 NR

Morning winds the summer out

Fresh kisses in the newest light

Sing hope and shout forever

Softly

We are mending pocket holes –

Lose a gem and stop to

Pick it up again sweet shining

Softly

Summer morning heals old wounds

Fresh wins sing away the doubt

Music born in touching you

Kisses and sparkles hope

Softly

Softly

29 July 1974

THE MAD POET

The mad poet works

Without sun, without light

His struggle with darkness

Extends through black night

The curtains are leaden

And parting the veil,

Is death to the fingers ....

And hard on his tale.

30 December 1974

Transmit True and Brightly

Edge of Fitchburg

Transmit True and Brightly

SKY CYCLE

The open heart

Receives the misty star

That smiles upon these ancient

Waiting brows.

The galaxies that swing the earth

Will wait upon us now

If we can only sing

And Heal

And sparkle back.

5 April 1975
NS

CLOUDS

Soft weeping siblings windward –
Such clouds cry Summer free,
And brothers in the morning
Float out so silvery.

My mist responds in mourning...
Not vexed, sweet clouds have come;
But know how brief their mooring,
And swift the dying hum.

11 July 1975
NS

A salute to human lifetimes

WITH CHILD

There are songs in me

And unknown dances,

Fiery in the Autumn winds,

And Wintery crystal dreams.

I'm pregnant with a poem so rare -

It will not yet be born

Because I'm busy gardening and harvesting,

Waiting

For the wild grapes to purple up,

Waiting for the jam to gel,

Waiting for the solstice and the equinox,

Living many songs,

Dancing all the dances in between,

Waiting for the poem

To live.

12 October 1975
NS

BILL

Now in November

Of your fiftieth year

You bring me spring

In all the glorious lights

And hope of warmth

You freely radiate

I praise the song that lives

In you ….

Applaud your spring

And fifty summer suns.

10 November 1975

Love, love, love

Nancy – your grateful wife

Now our star so close,

May we not see Spring

And linger on the gold in us

And not each others rust?

Raw gold was meant for polishing,

Raw stars for circling...

And we were meant to see the sky

Augmenting and diminishing.

                                        Today, 1975, 29 Decembre
                                        Ns

"O maun ha'e we the gift 'e gi'e us,
  To see ourselves as ithers see us!"
                            -Robert Burns-

$$E = MC^2$$

What light can move between our songs?

All the light that sings.

What songs can brighten shadow paths?

All our music shines.

You have given me to me;

All your giving glows.

Love's a star

And sparkling,

Never out of reach.

the last day of the year 1975
for Bill again
NS

WIZARD-BORN

The wizard-born have known

The music in the stars

And since their births have seen

The star that shines on them.

They recognize the stars that shine in other men

And recognize the shadows.

The wizard-born can sing

The songs of other hearts

And travel starry miles

Completing

Harmony.

31 December 1975
NS

MORNING STAR

I am the bright and

Morning star -

I am the only star you need.

The mystery that

Made yourself

Made me.

Remember me in longer years.

Remember dreamy mornings.

I sparkle in a part of you,

You shine in part of me.

14 January 1976
NS

Wanton shadows gleefully

Play upon the path behind.

All I see are whisperings,

Light and azure trails.

Valleys can"t consume my step,

Resting places for to drink.

"Come unto the mountain, child.",

My friend calls to me.

And I echo joyfully,

Thrusting forces birthing me,

Upward stony paths combine

To the breathing place.

And I query wistfully,

"Must I know you now, my sire?"

"Upward," (answer) "now you go."

Higher, higher,

Higher.

17 August 1976

Opening of the flowers within,

Summer of my series

Shines pure through petals of the past -

An August evolution.

Ablaze as jewels in a crown

Give life to every center

These flowers spin the earth around

If earth will let them enter.

Seeds of grey and black unite

And flame into a crystal

That sings unto a throaty blue

And flashes heart-borne scarlet.

Sunny solar plexus calls

And catches all the yellow;

From sparkling deep, the violet gem

Is womb of all the mothers.

Coccyx emeralds glisten true,

Radiant for returning

All the life-buds on the way -

Gem seeds brightly burning.

8-17-76

August Brilliant

August brilliant loneliness,
Light returns, I know.
It vacillates on thunderheads
And woos November snow.

Gardens greening in the sun,
Woods and shadows near,
Foods and fruits are ripening –
Lover, will you hear?

I can live the loneliness,
Lone, can love the dawn,
My love's snow can melt in me,
Shadows flash and gone.

Only hope his seed took root,
Blossoming his light,
So I might embrace that fruit
Safe from frosted night.

My love freezes loving now,

Not without a flaw –

My only August loneliness

Dies brilliant in the thaw.

17 August 1976

(hand written on back of August Brilliant)

Dear Kids,

I just must

Get away of a while.

Please understand –

I'll be back to get

You –

I really love you

Mom

ANSWER the PHONE! Please!!

From Luna to Sol

Lord of tomatoes and

Nuts in the shell

And all the bright zinnias,

You open the day.

Will you please give me a

Cloud-piercing yell

(To soothe my wild dark

  when I'm lost in the why)?

If you can see me through all of your mist-

-Maybe you'll finally know you exist!

Maybe you'll meet with more

Lights on the way,

Merging your glow with the

Blaze of the sky.

21 August 1976

Light Song

Light,

I need your cadences

Not only from the gold and silver harmonies

Reflecting far,

But from your ancient fingerings

And human song to me.

I need your special octave of

The glow,

I need your symphonies in tune,

I need your melody.

21 August 1976

Transmit True and Brightly

PROVERB

If one human song

Would clash with yours,

It does not mean that he

Is out of tune.

It does not mean that you

 Are out of tune.

  Two different keys,

   And each completing harmony,

    That's all it is.

8 September 1976

Angels sleep in

Every cring&ing element

That fiery dawn

Lights up in wondering.

And if I turn

A tear into a rainbow drop,

Then angels wake

And keep their destiny.

8 September 1976

Peter Piper

So much for pickled pencils!

I don't enjoy the dill

And peppers sown among the

Dreaming children.

I wish to challenge

Every judge who sits

Upon a sweet and sour

Testing of the soul,

And now allow

The ones who come from in me

To speak their spicy wares

And not forget the salt.

8 Sptmbr 1976

Trust

I trust old sunrises,

Pages that musted,

Moonbeams that turn my hope,

Trunks that are crusted

With time. And I trust the Earth,

Ancient and busted,

Dreamers who scanned the skies

When the stars lusted.

Truth filters from the dream,

Corny and rusted -

People who cannot trust

Cannot be trusted.

8 September 1976

Transmit True and Brightly

Phoenix

What would I give

To see this planet

Rise Anew

With ancient strength

And newly golden wings

To birth within itself

The flashing of a million stars –

An octave of

The universe that

Gave it

Self!

8 September 1976

To Dara

I know some things of daughtering

And how you feel to grow –

But how I touch a growing one

Or how I touch the wind

Is still an unborn song.

20 September 1976

Your mystery still

Resided in me

Because we made a

Secret contract

Long before we lived

And now your shadow

Finds another home

But not for light.

And lasting music

Sings you

To my

Shine.

21 September 1976

My only hope is now avoiding

Darking things,

And yet I grapple

Unknown demons piercing in,

And quagmires call my other self

To fates obscured by

Dragon breath.

And when I activate

The monster sleeping dream,

I bring to waking times

The sorrow of my shine.

Tomorrow radiates a quickening

Between the changeing skies

And sparkling wofilds

That vanishing

Only offer time.

24 September 1976

To a Friend

One journey last,
Conceived in wind and flame
To sail a soul
To realms
Where love can call
A sunbeam to the heart. - -
And from ~~the~~ your ancient rigging
Peace now fills ~~the~~
Old sails,
Rejoice!
For you have tasted
Salt upon ~~their~~ the prow
And in the
Wildest ports.

1 October 1976

To a Friend

One journey last,

Conceived in wind and flame

To sail a soul

To realms

Where love can call

A sunbeam to the heart.

And from your ancient rigging

Peace now fills

Old sails.

Rejoice!

For you have tasted

Salt upon the prow

And in the

Wildest ports.

1 October 1976

Places of Light

Transmit True and Brightly

To stand in crystal solitude

And send a golden ray

Rainbow riding.

Glancing, gliding

Out into the day

To transmit true and brightly

All light that shows

That you are there.

Miriam 1980

I was baptized in infancy

Nancy Jean or "Anna John"

In Latin as used by the

RC church. Upon my

Baptism into the Orthodox American

Church in 1969 I was quite

Willing to use the Hebrew form

Of Nancy (or Anna) which is Hannah.

But after looking over a list

Of Orthodox names, one name

Popped out at me and I

Recognized it as my True Name

Miriam

January 1980

I am the bright and

Morning star.

I am the only

Star you need.

The mystery that made

Yourself

Made me.

Remember me in planet nights

In distant starless windings,

I sparkle in a part

Of you –

You shine in part

Of me.

Miriam

From Terra

Light, I need your cadences

Not only from the

Gold and silver harmonies

Reflecting far

But from your ancient fingerings

And human song to me.

I need your special octave

Of the fire glow

I need your melody

Man –

I need

Your tune.

Spinning sweet from fire to water

In the center there is calm

Wheels in wheels, transfiguration,

First fruits come to altar home

Stand in awe, reveal the splendor

Strew the path of heart ablaze

With the flowers, plums of summer,

Walk the cliff with upward gaze

Kneel before the King of Rainbows

You are now a Child of Light

Called to stillness in the wind rush

Quietly an eagle flight

Spinning sweet from fire to water
In the center there is calm
Wheels in wheels, ~~to high consciou~~
Transfiguration,
First fruits come to altar home

Stand in awe, reveal the splendor
Strew the path of heart ablaze
With the flowers, plums of Summer,
Walk the cliff with upward gaze

Kneel before the King of Rainbows
You are now a Child of Light
Called to stillness in the wind rush
Quietly an eagle flight.

Beneath the wings of Quetzlcoatl

In the mountain city of Tenochtitlan

Mercury rose before the Light

To tell the sky of Life

So early torn from Dark

Deep in the womb.

Red Rivers ran before my eyes

A heavenly decision made

To stay on earth this time –

And then first breath

Soft Ancient Cry

Sun-Child met the dawn.

22 May 1961

Mexico City, D.F.

(sent in birthday card 5/22/91)

Ash Wednesday

Echoing the ancient music

Somewhere in the recesses of Time

Ashes blessed by Holiness

In simple earthen ware

Are signed upon the foreheads

Of our souls

And we remember:

Dust we are and spirit soup

Sent by seraphim and lengthening days

As we begin our journey to the Light

The sun begins its Northering –

A gift from Heaven in the tents

That cover holiness

As do our sacred bodies

Cover sacred souls –

And I remember Holiness and dust

Whenever your tent touches mines –

The open flaps that let the sunrise in,

Or even snowflakes sparkling in the night

Forever call me to you tent.

Forever will I come.

Forever will this sanctity

    Unite our sacred bodies

    Containing sacred spirits

    Pure and Holy

    In the dust

1991

An innocent and holy love in August

Reborn without a stain

United us

Invited us to keep a sacred channel

[The river changing us forever]

Running free to starlight mansions

A pure angelic union dropped upon us

From Heaven in the power of the Light

Will we accept a life of crystal rainbows,

Transforming the mundane to what can Be?

Or will we simply show each other

Feathered souvenirs and memories,

Display and pack away again unchanged

Our incenses and colored lights and lifetimes

And sadly speak of what we might have been

Had not world of form attracted us

So warmly

Had not the Earth enticed us to her

Breast

Can we accept a life of crystal rainbows

Transmit True and Brightly

When Earth call us so warmly to her Breast?

Can we refuse to keep a sacred channel

When Pure and Holy Light keeps us alive?

"A sleeping body scattereth at the same time soweth."

Words heard as I awoke from a dream this morning. I was being shown my sleeping body as the words were spoken.

Some days, like today, I am Your completely empty dark chalice waiting. For You, only You, sweet Lord.

M (Miriam)

From Journal notes

Transmit True and Brightly

Epilogue:

Nancy - 6 months - Your eyes are so beautiful. Even then,
they seemed to know what it's all about.   (written on the back of
an old photo)

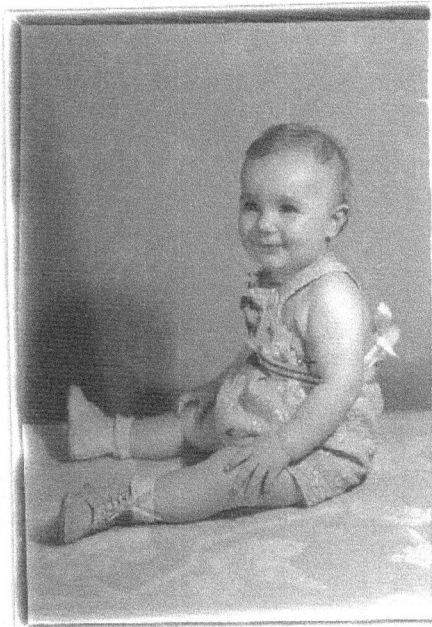

Transmit True and Brightly

Index

By Title / First Line

Transmit True and Brightly

www.ingramcontent.com/pod-product-compliance
Lightning Source LLC
La Vergne TN
LVHW011347080426
835511LV00005B/174